Contents

What is a screw?   4
What does a screw do?   6
How does a screw work?   8
Nuts and bolts   10
Screws for holding   12
Screws for drilling   14
Screws for gripping   16
Screws for squashing   18
Screws for lifting   20
Screws for moving   22
Adjusting with screws   24
Screws in machines   26
Amazing screw facts   28
Glossary   30
More books to read   32
Index   32

Any words appearing in the text in bold, **like this**, are explained in the Glossary.

What is a screw?

A machine is a man-made **device**. Machines make our lives easier by helping us to do jobs. This hook has a simple machine on the end. It is called a **screw**.

screw

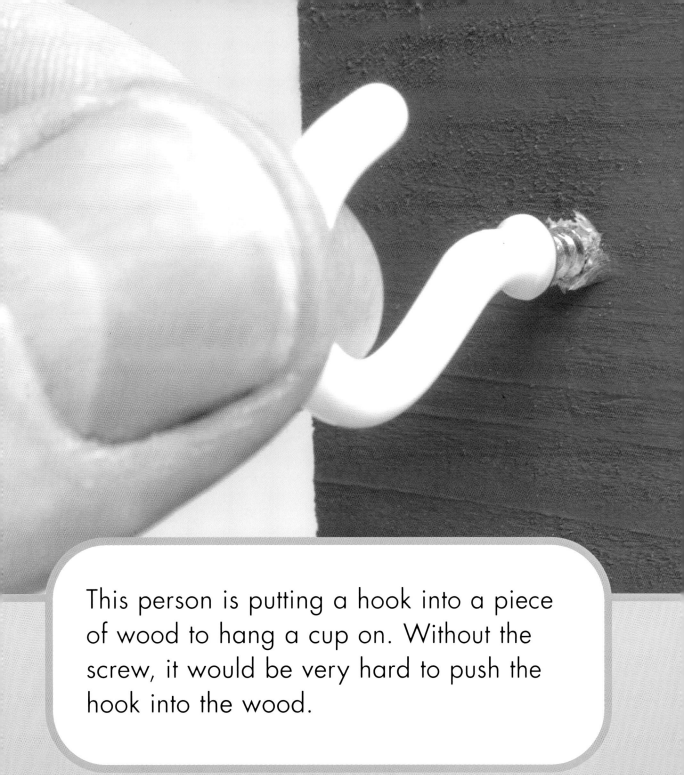

This person is putting a hook into a piece of wood to hang a cup on. Without the screw, it would be very hard to push the hook into the wood.

What does a screw do?

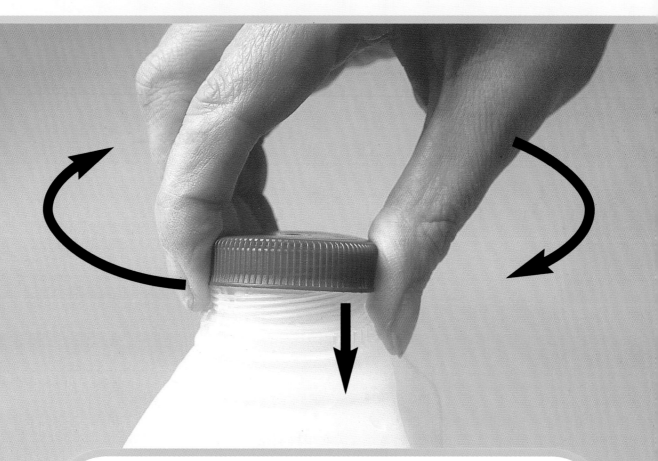

When a **screw** is turned, it changes a movement in one direction into movement in another direction. Turning this bottle cap makes it move up or down.

We also use screws for fixing and holding things. This light bulb has a metal screw. Turning the light bulb moves it into the holder. The screw holds the bulb in place.

How does a screw work?

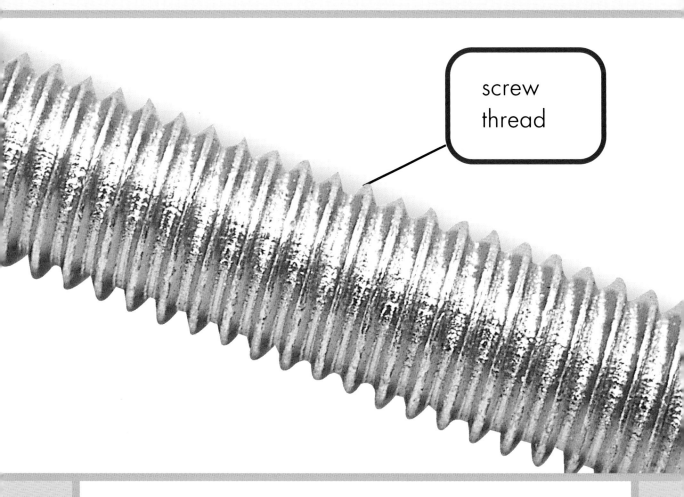

screw thread

A **screw** is made up of a piece of material with a **groove** around the outside. The groove is called a **screw thread**. Here is a close-up picture of a screw thread.

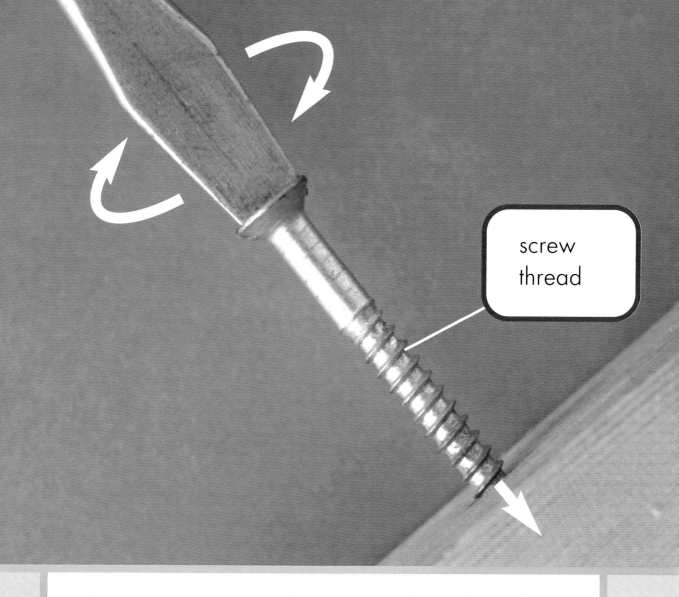

screw
thread

As a screw turns, the screw thread pushes
against a piece of material or against
another screw thread. This makes the
screw move.

Nuts and bolts

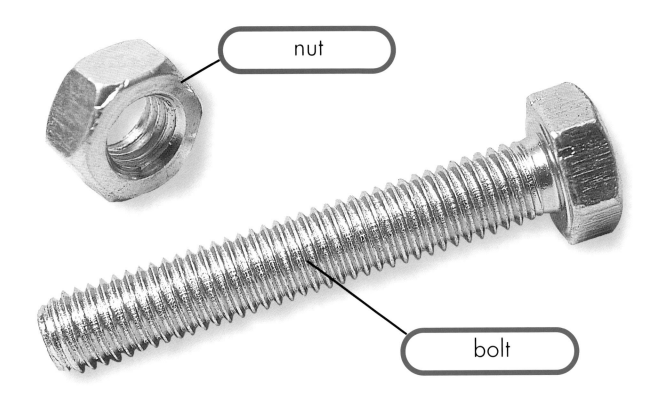

nut

bolt

Nuts and **bolts** always work together.
A bolt has a **screw thread** on the
outside. A nut has one on the inside.
Turning a nut makes it move along a bolt.

bolt

We join things together with nuts and bolts. You put the bolt through holes in the objects and turn the nut with a **spanner**. This pulls the objects firmly together.

Screws for holding

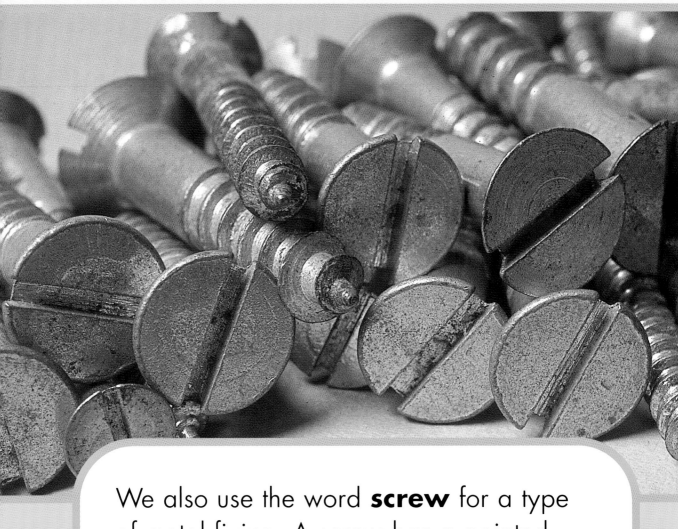

We also use the word **screw** for a type of metal fixing. A screw has a pointed end and a **screw thread**. These screws are for fixing things to wood.

As a screw turns, it moves further into the wood. When the screw is completely in, turning it more pulls the numberplate tighter against the door. Now the numberplate cannot move.

Screws for drilling

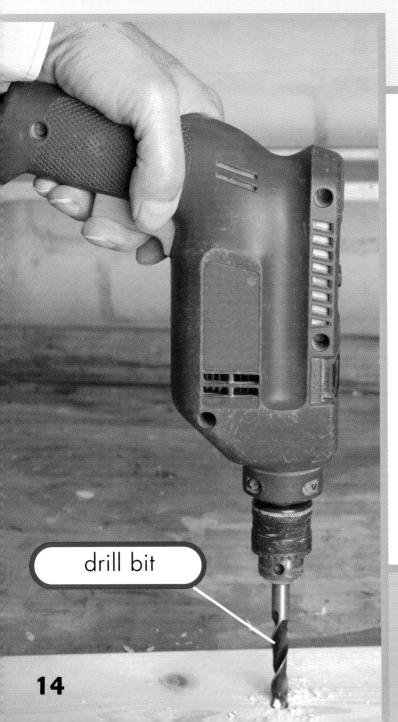

drill bit

We also use **screws** for drilling holes. The **drill bit** on this drill has a **screw thread**. The end cuts into the wood. The screw thread pushes the waste wood out of the hole it has made.

Here is another type of screw for drilling. An auger is like a giant drill bit. Fishermen use an auger to drill holes in the ice, so they can catch fish.

Screws for gripping

We also use **screws** for gripping things tightly. This **device** is called a clamp. Tightening the clamp makes the screw move until it holds the pieces of wood firmly together.

A vice is like a clamp. It holds an object still while you drill or cut it. Turning the handle makes screws pull the two sides of the vice together.

Screws for squashing

Turning a **screw** makes a big push. So screws are good for squashing things. This is a screw press. Turning the handle squashes the fruit inside to get the juice out.

Inside a plastic bottle top is a plastic **disc**. When the top is screwed on, it squashes the disc to make an **airtight seal**. This stops the drink going flat.

Screws for lifting

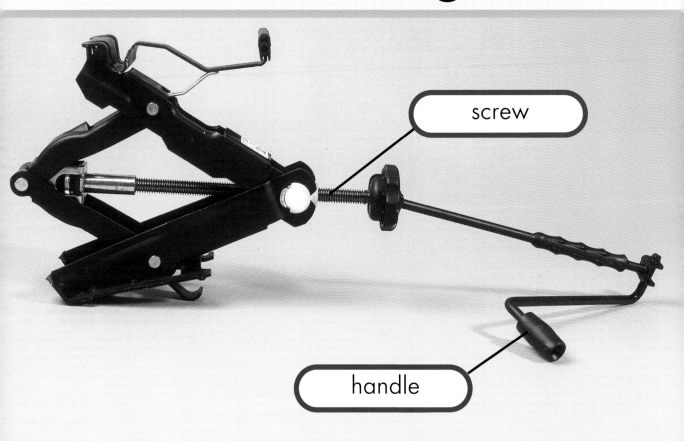

screw

handle

We use **screws** for lifting and supporting objects. A jack is a **device** for lifting a car. Across the middle is a very long screw with a handle on the end.

Turning the jack's handle pulls the two sides of the jack together. The jack pushes up on the car. The screw means that a small push on the handle lifts the heavy car.

Screws for moving

propeller

If we spin a screw round, it can make things move. A boat **propeller** is like a big screw. When it turns, it pushes water backwards, which pushes the boat forwards.

This electric fan has fan blades shaped like a large **screw thread**. When the electric **motor** turns the blades, they push air forwards. The moving air cools the room.

Adjusting with screws

screw thread
under seat

Each turn of a **screw** only makes the screw move backwards or forwards a tiny bit. Turning the seat of this stool makes it move up or down slightly.

You have to **focus** a **microscope** to see the object clearly. The focus knob is a screw. Turning it slowly makes the microscope's tube move up or down just a tiny bit. This makes it easy to focus.

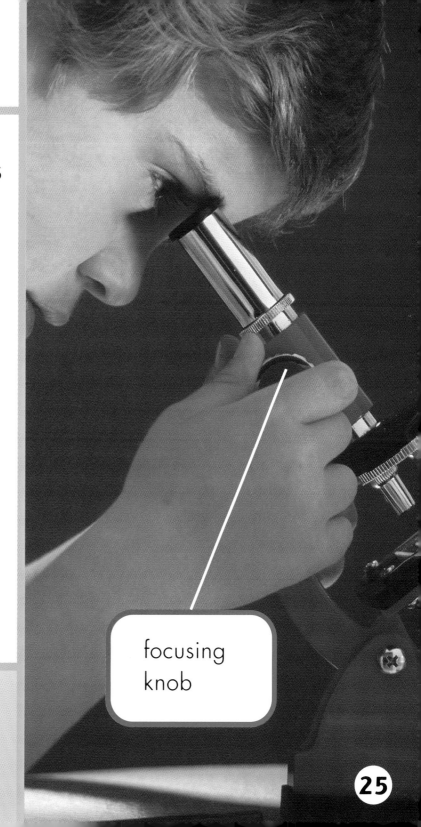

focusing knob

Screws in machines

screw

screw

Hundreds of complicated machines have **screws** inside that help them to work. Most machines, like this robot head, are held together by dozens of screws and **nuts** and **bolts**.

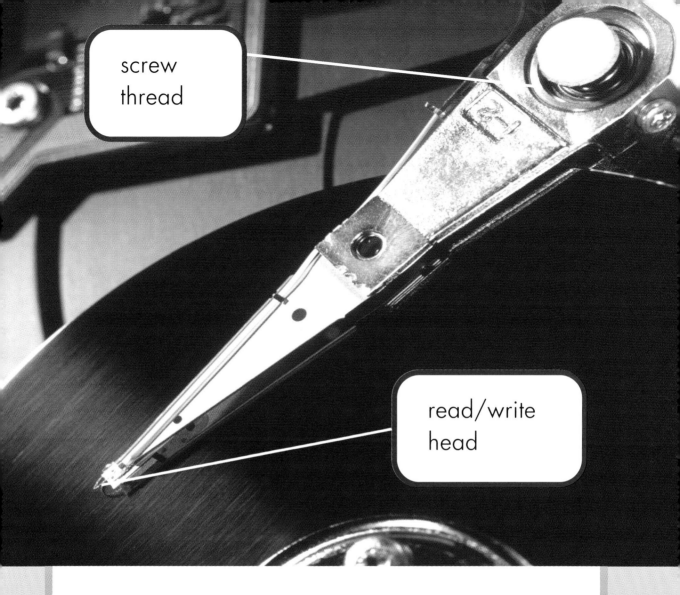

screw
thread

read/write
head

This is the inside of a computer's **disc drive**. The tiny **screw thread** moves the reading and writing **head** backwards and forwards across the disc.

Amazing screw facts

- The **screw** is one of the oldest machines in the world. It was invented in Greece more than 2000 years ago.
- An Archimedean screw is a long tube with a **screw thread** inside. In some places in the world it is used for lifting water from rivers on to fields.
- The first ship **propellers** were made nearly 200 years ago. They were called screws instead of propellers because they were shaped like huge screws.
- Scientists and **engineers** use screws for measuring things very accurately. They use a **device** called a micrometer screw gauge.

- Engineers use very big strong **nuts** and **bolts** to join the parts of a building frame together.

Glossary

airtight	stops air getting in or out
bolt	rod with a screw thread around the outside
device	thing that does a job. A clothes peg is a device. So is an electronic calculator.
disc	round, flat piece of material
disc drive	machine in a computer that stores information
drill bit	metal rod that fits into a drill and cuts a hole
engineer	person who designs, makes or mends machines
focus	to make an image sharp and clear
groove	long, very narrow hole
head	in a disc drive, part that reads or records data on to a disc

microscope	device that makes tiny objects look much bigger
motor	machine that turns power into movement
nut	square or hexagonal (six-sided) piece of material with a hole in the middle and a screw thread inside
propeller	object that pushes water or air when it spins round
screw	simple machine or a type of fixing with a screw thread around the outside and a sharp tip
screw thread	groove around the outside of a screw or bolt
seal	piece of material that stops water or air getting through a hole
spanner	tool for turning nuts or bolts

More books to read

What do Screws do?, David Glover (Heinemann Library, 1996)

Screws, Angela Royston (Heinemann Library, 2000)

What is a Screw?, Lloyd G. Douglas (Children's Press, 2002)

What are Screws?, Helen Frost (Pebble Books, 2001)

Index

adjusting things 24–5
Archimedean screw 28
disc drive 27
drilling holes 14–15
fixing and holding 7, 11, 12–13, 29
gripping 16–17
hooks 4, 5
jack 20–1
lifting and supporting things 20–1

machines 4, 26–7, 28
measuring things 28
microscope 25
moving things 22–3
nuts and bolts 10–11, 26, 29
propellers 22, 28
screw thread 8–9, 10, 12, 14, 23, 27, 28
squashing things 18–19